The Big Book of
DINOSAURS

DK UK

Project editor Sam Priddy
Project art editor Fiona Macdonald
Designer Jim Green
Additional illustrators Arran Lewis, Simon Mumford
Senior producer, Pre-production Francesca Wardell
Senior producers Andrew Beehag, Srijana Gurung
Managing editor Laura Gilbert
Managing art editor Diane Peyton Jones
Publisher Sarah Larter
Publishing director Sophie Mitchell

DK India

Senior editor Shatarupa Chaudhuri
Project editor Suneha Dutta
Art editor Shreya Sadhan
Assistant art editor Kartik Gera
DTP designers Bimlesh Tiwary, Jagtar Singh
Managing editor Alka Thakur Hazarika
Senior managing art editor Romi Chakraborty
CTS manager Balwant Singh
Production manager Pankaj Sharma
Picture researcher Sumedha Chopra

Original editor Lara Tankel Holtz
Original designer Mary Sandberg

This revised edition published in 2019
First published in Great Britain in 1994 by
Dorling Kindersley Limited
80 Strand, London WC2R 0RL

Copyright © 1994, 2019 Dorling Kindersley Limited
A Penguin Random House Company
10 9 8 7 6 5 4 3 2 1
001-259187-May/2019

A CIP catalogue record for this book is available from the British Library.
ISBN: 978-0-2414-0087-6

Printed and bound in China.

A WORLD OF IDEAS:
SEE ALL THERE IS TO KNOW

www.dk.com

DORLING KINDERSLEY would like to thank Olivia Stanford for proofreading.

The publisher would like to thank the following for their kind permission to reproduce their photographs: (Key: a-above; b-below/bottom; c-centre; f-far; l-left; r-right; t-top)
4-5 Dorling Kindersley: Senckenberg Nature Museum, Frankfurt (bc). **4 Dorling Kindersley:** The American Museum of Natural History (c); Natural History Museum, London (tr, cla); Peter Minister (clb). **6 Dorling Kindersley:** The American Museum of Natural History (tr). **6-7 Dorling Kindersley:** Senckenberg Gesellschaft Fuer Naturforschugn Museum. **11 Dorling Kindersley:** Natural History Museum, London (bl); Royal Tyrrell Museum of Palaeontology, Alberta, Canada (clb). **12 Dorling Kindersley:** Royal Tyrrell Museum of Palaeontology, Alberta, Canada (t). **13 Dorling Kindersley:** Royal Tyrrell Museum of Palaeontology, Alberta, Canada (bl). **Science Photo Library:** Julius T Csotonyi (br). **14 Dorling Kindersley:** Natural History Museum, London (cra). **15 Dorling Kindersley:** Natural History Museum, London (cl); Staatliches Museum fur Naturkunde Stuttgart (tr); Royal Tyrrell Museum of Palaeontology, Alberta, Canada (bl). **16 Getty Images:** Arthur Dorety / Stocktrek Images (br). **18 Dorling Kindersley:** Carnegie Museum of Natural History, Pittsburgh (tl). **20 Dorling Kindersley:** Queensland Museum, Brisbane, Australia (cla). **21 Dorling Kindersley:** Royal Tyrrell Museum of Palaeontology, Alberta, Canada (br). **22 Dorling Kindersley:** Senckenberg Nature Museum, Frankfurt (bl). **23 Dorling Kindersley:** Natural History Museum, London (c). **25 Dorling Kindersley:** Natural History Museum, London (cl); Senckenberg Nature Museum, Frankfurt (tr). **26 Dorling Kindersley:** Royal Tyrrell Museum of Palaeontology, Alberta, Canada (bl). **28 Dorling Kindersley:** The American Museum of Natural History (tl). **29 Dorling Kindersley:** Royal Tyrrell Museum of Palaeontology, Alberta, Canada (tr). **31 Dorling Kindersley:** Jon Hughes (tl). **32-33 Fotolia:** Michael Rosskothen (bc). **32 Getty Images:** Spencer Platt (cl). **39 Dorling Kindersley:** Natural History Museum, London (bl). **40 Dorling Kindersley:** Jon Hughes (br). **42 Dorling Kindersley:** Natural History Museum, London (b). **The Natural History Museum, London:** (cl). **43 Corbis:** Sergey Krasovskiy / Stocktrek Images (t). **Dorling Kindersley:** Natural History Museum, London (br). **44 Corbis:** Corey Ford / Stocktrek Images (bc). **Dorling Kindersley:** Natural History Museum, London (br). **James St. John (Ohio State University at Newark)** (tl). **45 Dreamstime.com:** Corey A. Ford (tl). © **2012 Longrich, Field:** Longrich NR, Field DJ (2012) Torosaurus Is Not Triceratops: Ontogeny in Chasmosaurine Ceratopsids as a Case Study in Dinosaur Taxonomy. PLoS ONE 7(2): e32623. doi:10.1371/journal.pone.0032623 (distributed under the terms of the Creative Commons Attribution License: http://creativecommons.org/licenses/by/2.5/) (bl, br).
Cover images: Front: **Dreamstime.com:** Aleksander Bedrin (br), Panaceadoll (c/) (Background).

All other images © Dorling Kindersley
For further information see: www.dkimages.com

The Big Book of
DINOSAURS

Written by
Angela Wilkes and Darren Naish

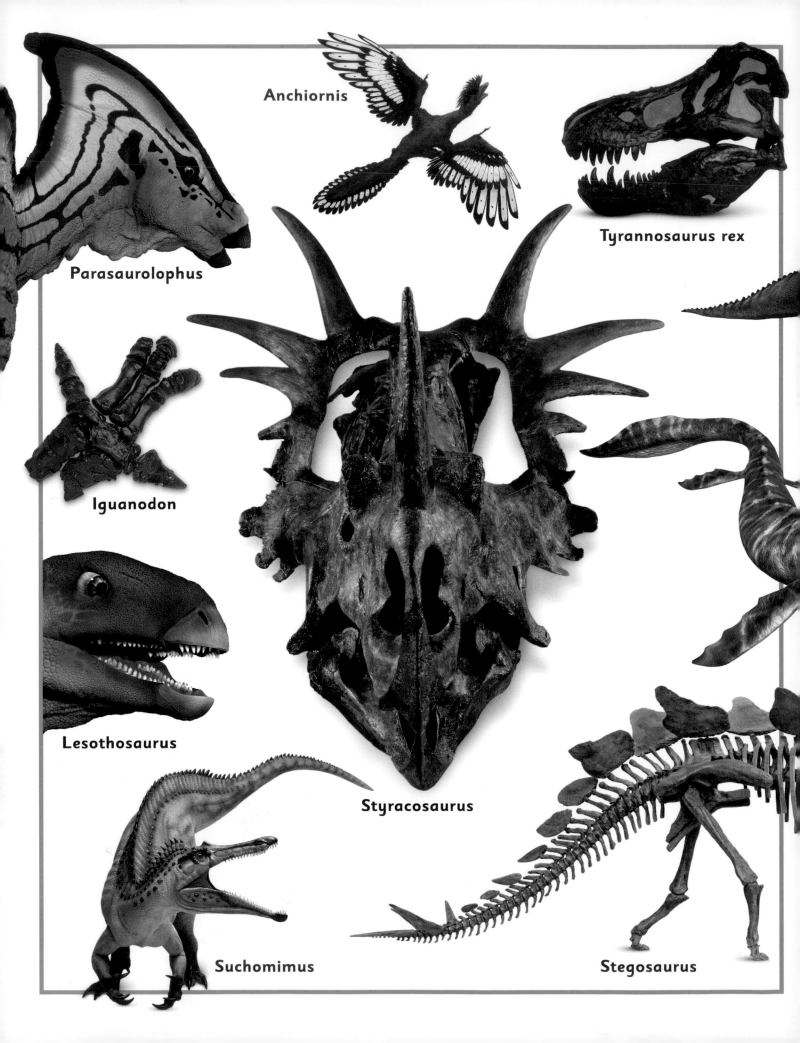

Anchiornis

Tyrannosaurus rex

Parasaurolophus

Iguanodon

Lesothosaurus

Styracosaurus

Suchomimus

Stegosaurus

Contents

Ceratosaurus

Eoraptor

Triceratops

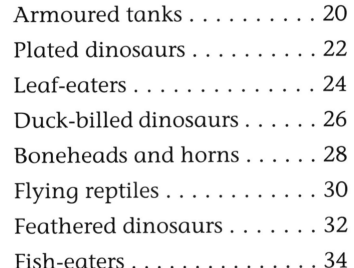

Mosasaurus

Saltasaurus

Dinosaur clues

Clues to the past

How do we know so much about dinosaurs when the last ones died millions and millions of years ago? Scientists hunt for the fossil remains of dinosaur bones and teeth, buried in rocks. They use these clues to find out as much as they can about dinosaurs.

This hole shows where the dinosaur's eye was

Tyrannosaurus rex skull

Heavy tail helped to balance the body

Tyrannosaurus rex's huge jaw and sharp teeth show that it was a fierce meat-eater

Tail bones

Strong legs

Rebuilding a dinosaur

Scientists can fit together a dinosaur's fossil bones to build a life-size skeleton, like the Tyrannosaurus rex here. They usually make models of any bones that are missing.

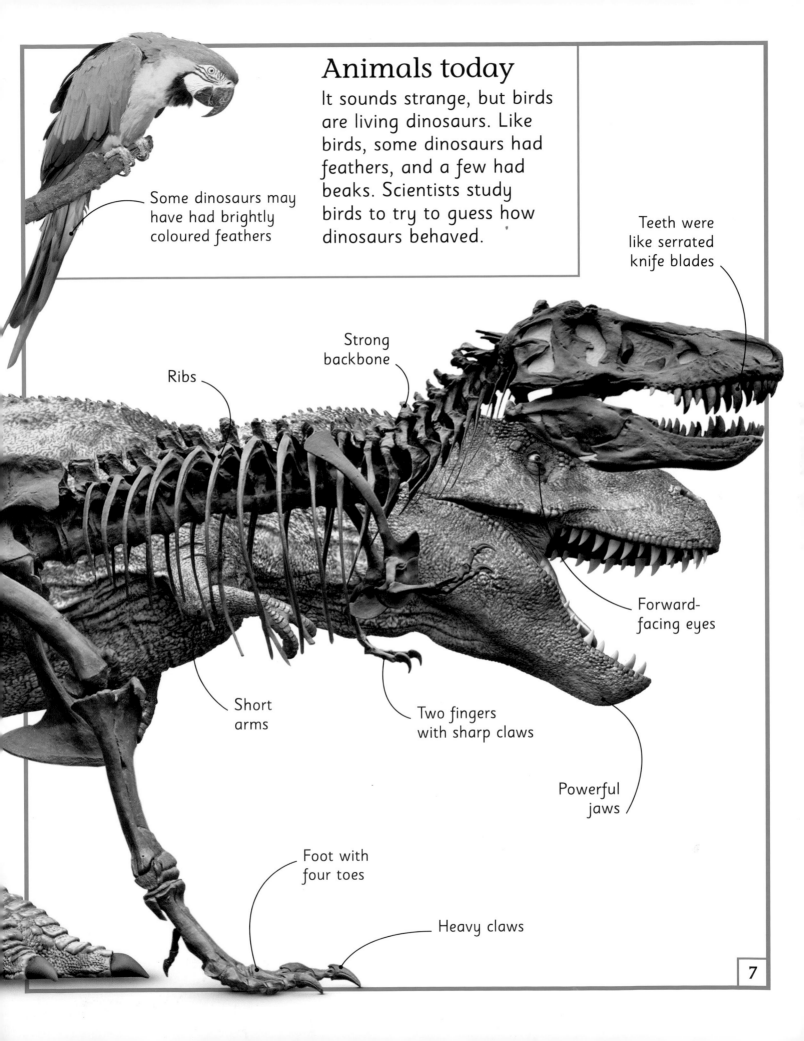

Animals today

It sounds strange, but birds are living dinosaurs. Like birds, some dinosaurs had feathers, and a few had beaks. Scientists study birds to try to guess how dinosaurs behaved.

Some dinosaurs may have had brightly coloured feathers

Teeth were like serrated knife blades

Strong backbone

Ribs

Forward-facing eyes

Short arms

Two fingers with sharp claws

Powerful jaws

Foot with four toes

Heavy claws

Face to face

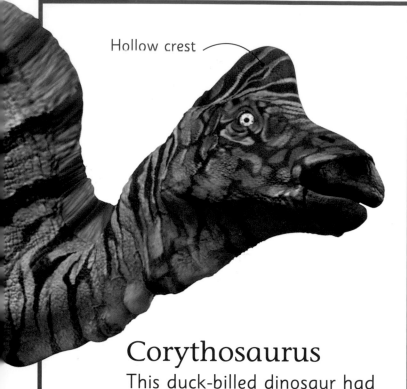

Hollow crest

Euoplocephalus

Euoplocephalus was an armoured dinosaur covered in bony lumps and bumps.

Triceratops

This big plant-eater had a head frill and three sharp horns.

Corythosaurus

This duck-billed dinosaur had a crest on its head that looked like a plate standing on edge.

Stegosaurus

This plant-eater had two rows of plates along its back and spikes on its tail, which were used for defence.

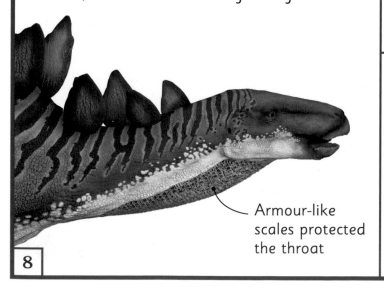

Armour-like scales protected the throat

Citipati

Citipati had a strong, parrot-like beak and a large crest on its head.

Citipati was covered in feathers

Teeth at the front of
the jaw helped to
rip leaves

Barosaurus

This gigantic
plant-eater had
a neck more than
9 m (30 ft) long.

Alxasaurus had
a long neck

Alxasaurus

This dinosaur from China was
covered in downy feathers.

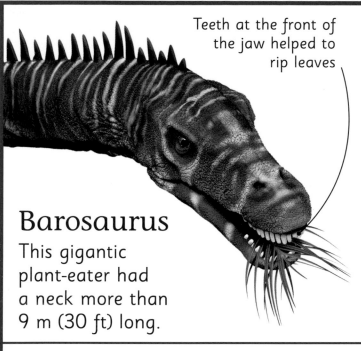

Edmontonia

Edmontonia had a
tough armour of bony
plates and fierce spikes,
which it used
when charging
at enemies. It
mainly ate moss
and ferns.

Lesothosaurus

This small and light dinosaur could run
very fast, and so could get away from
its enemies quickly. It had big eyes,
which gave it an all-round
view. This meant
it could spot
danger
easily.

Crown of
small spikes

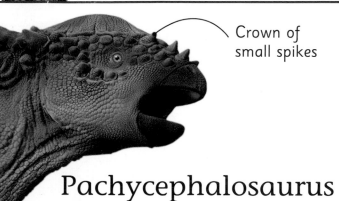

Pachycephalosaurus

This dinosaur had a strange,
bony head that looked like
a crash helmet.

Iguanodon

Iguanodon was a
big, plant-eating
dinosaur with
lots of strong
teeth.

Fast and fierce

Deinonychus

Deinonychus was a fast and very fierce dinosaur. It pinned its victims down on the ground with the long, curved claws on its feet. It used its razor-sharp teeth to tear off chunks of flesh.

Deinonychus had 70 jagged teeth, which helped it to eat tough meat

Flexible, bird-like neck

Troodon's eyes faced forwards

Troodon

This quick-witted dinosaur had a brain that was bigger than that of most dinosaurs. Its large eyes helped it to hunt for prey at night.

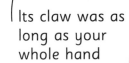

Its claw was as long as your whole hand

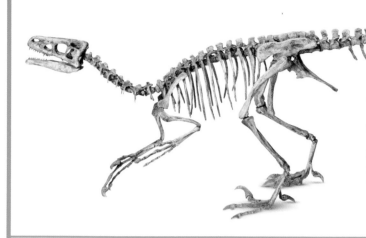

Ornitholestes

Ornitholestes was light and speedy, and had a very long tail. It probably hunted small reptiles.

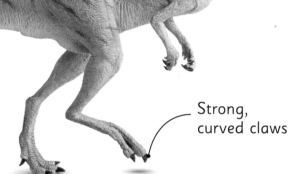

Herrerasaurus used its long tail to stay balanced

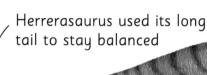

Herrerasaurus

Herrerasaurus was one of the first dinosaurs, living 225 million years ago. It was as long as a small car.

Strong, curved claws

Dromaeosaurus

This dinosaur's name means "running lizard". Dromaeosaurus was an active hunter. Its skull shows that it had powerful jaws lined with saw-edged teeth.

Compsognathus

Compsognathus lived 150 million years ago and was no bigger than a chicken. It could run very swiftly to catch small lizards and insects to eat.

Compsognathus had a narrow head

Beaky dinosaurs

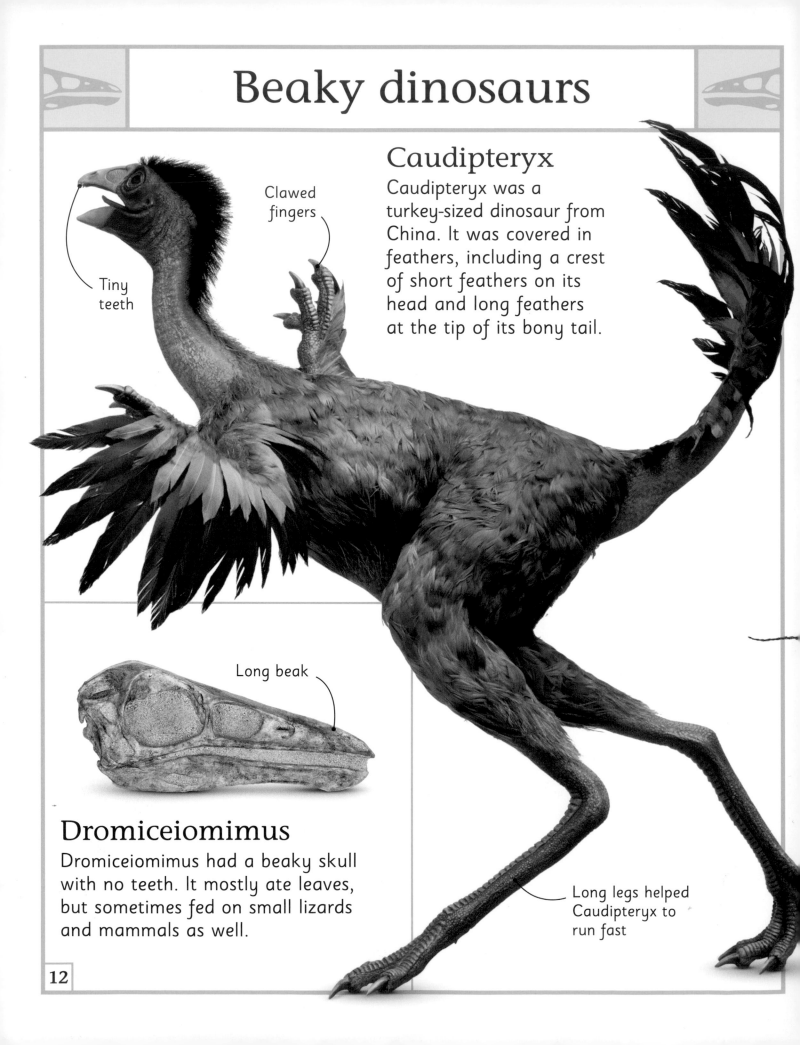

Tiny
teeth

Clawed
fingers

Caudipteryx

Caudipteryx was a
turkey-sized dinosaur from
China. It was covered in
feathers, including a crest
of short feathers on its
head and long feathers
at the tip of its bony tail.

Long beak

Dromiceiomimus

Dromiceiomimus had a beaky skull
with no teeth. It mostly ate leaves,
but sometimes fed on small lizards
and mammals as well.

Long legs helped
Caudipteryx to
run fast

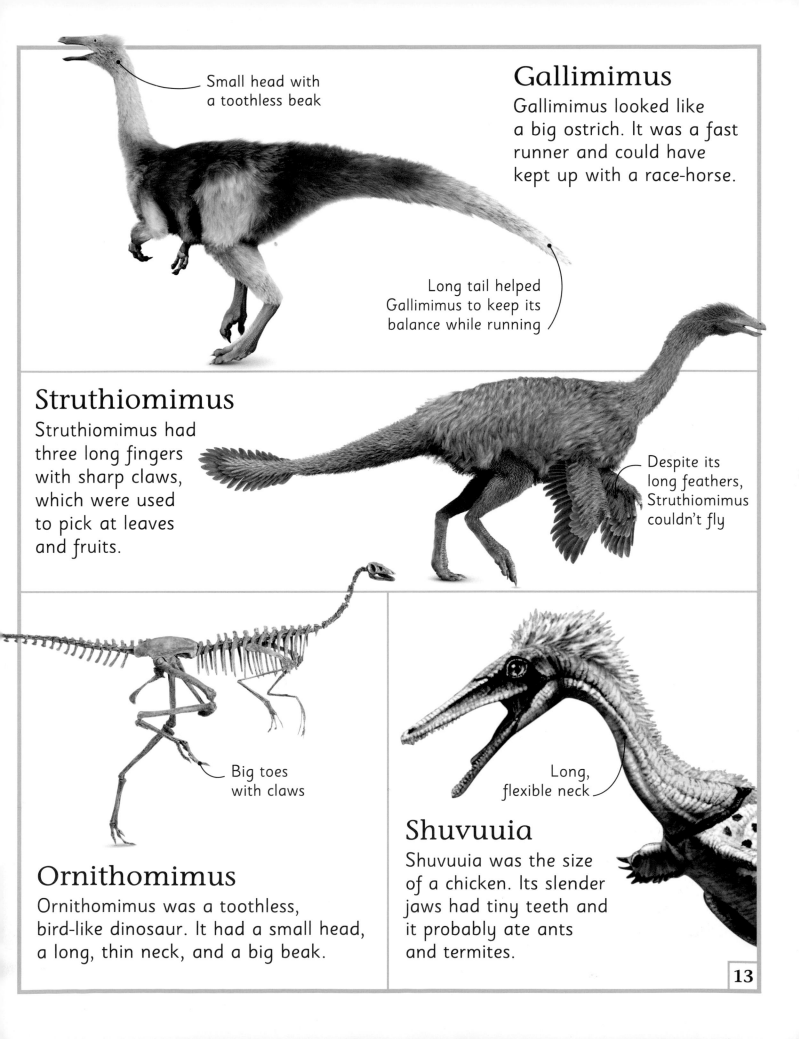

Small head with
a toothless beak

Gallimimus

Gallimimus looked like
a big ostrich. It was a fast
runner and could have
kept up with a race-horse.

Long tail helped
Gallimimus to keep its
balance while running

Struthiomimus

Struthiomimus had
three long fingers
with sharp claws,
which were used
to pick at leaves
and fruits.

Despite its
long feathers,
Struthiomimus
couldn't fly

Big toes
with claws

Long,
flexible neck

Shuvuuia

Shuvuuia was the size
of a chicken. Its slender
jaws had tiny teeth and
it probably ate ants
and termites.

Ornithomimus

Ornithomimus was a toothless,
bird-like dinosaur. It had a small head,
a long, thin neck, and a big beak.

13

Terrible teeth

Tyrannosaurus rex

Scientists can tell what kind of food an animal eats by looking at its teeth. Tyrannosaurus rex had huge jaws that could open very wide and long, sharp teeth.

Duriavenator

Duriavenator's teeth were curved like daggers. When a tooth broke or wore out, a new one grew in its place.

New tooth ready to come through

These jaws were strong enough to crush bones

Tyrannosaurus rex's teeth were as long as table knives

Allosaurus

Allosaurus was a savage meat-eater. Its teeth were sharp for slicing through flesh. They curved backwards to give Allosaurus a firm grip on its victims.

Blade-like teeth

Diplodocus

Diplodocus was an enormous plant-eater. It had thin teeth, like small pencils, for ripping leaves from branches.

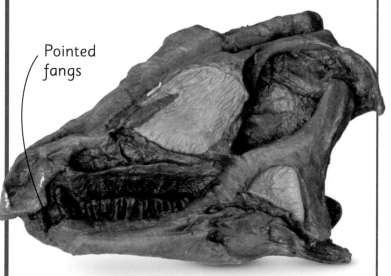

Pointed fangs

Heterodontosaurus

Heterodontosaurus was a plant-eater. It had a horny beak, and teeth for cutting and grinding leaves.

Curved teeth tore through flesh

Eoraptor

This little meat-eater had small, sharp teeth. It probably ate big insects and lizards.

15

Mighty meat-eaters

Sharp teeth

Short arms

Strong legs helped in chasing prey

Carnotaurus

The fiercest dinosaurs were the two-legged meat-eaters such as Carnotaurus. It hunted other dinosaurs or ate dead animals that it found.

Acrocanthosaurus

Acrocanthosaurus was a strong predator with knife-like teeth that could tear open tough skin.

Bony lumps above eyes

Massive jaws with rows of fangs

Long tail helped Acrocanthosaurus to keep balance

Tyrannosaurus rex

Tyrannosaurus was one of the biggest and strongest meat-eating animals ever — it was nearly as tall as a two-storey house. Although it was very heavy, scientists think it could sprint over short distances.

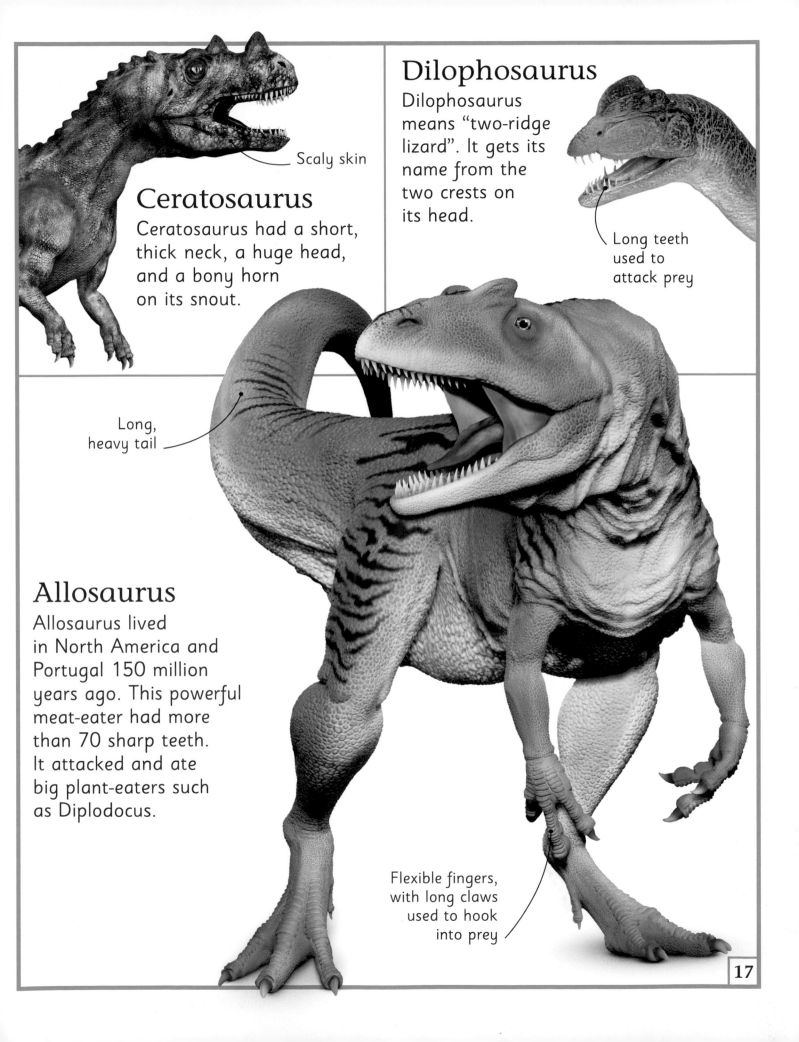

Ceratosaurus

Scaly skin

Ceratosaurus had a short, thick neck, a huge head, and a bony horn on its snout.

Dilophosaurus

Dilophosaurus means "two-ridge lizard". It gets its name from the two crests on its head.

Long teeth used to attack prey

Long, heavy tail

Allosaurus

Allosaurus lived in North America and Portugal 150 million years ago. This powerful meat-eater had more than 70 sharp teeth. It attacked and ate big plant-eaters such as Diplodocus.

Flexible fingers, with long claws used to hook into prey

17

Biggest on Earth

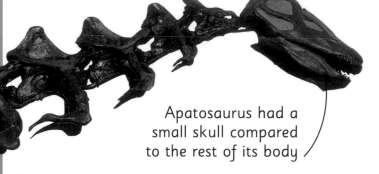

Apatosaurus

This dinosaur had peg-like teeth for stripping leaves from plants. Apatosaurus was so big, it probably had to spend most of the day eating.

Apatosaurus had a small skull compared to the rest of its body

Mamenchisaurus

Mamenchisaurus's neck grew up to 15 m (50 ft) long. That's nearly three times as long as a giraffe's neck.

The long, thin tail was carried off the ground

Argentinosaurus

Argentinosaurus was probably the heaviest dinosaur ever found. Scientists think it could have weighed as much as six fire engines.

Tough protective scales

Barosaurus had a strong, whip-like tail

Diplodocus

Diplodocus was the longest dinosaur of all. It was much longer than a tennis court. Despite its massive size, it only had a tiny brain.

Diplodocus stripped leaves off branches with its long, thin teeth

Saltasaurus

Saltasaurus's back and sides were protected by bony plates and lumps beneath its skin.

Saltasaurus's tough skin made it hard for predators to eat it

Barosaurus's heavy neck was held up by strong bones

Barosaurus

Barosaurus was one of the tallest dinosaurs. It could reach treetops as high as a five-storey building.

19

Minmi

Minmi was a small dinosaur that lived in Australia. It was so well-protected that it had bony plates on its belly as well as its back.

Horned head

Turtle-shaped head

Short, stocky limbs

Gargoyleosaurus

Gargoyleosaurus had seven teeth at the front of its jaw, which it used to tear leaves and stems off plants.

Its eyelids were covered with small plates

Ankylosaurus

Ankylosaurus was a huge dinosaur, as big as a car, protected by bony plates. It was armed with a club on its tail, which it swung at its attackers.

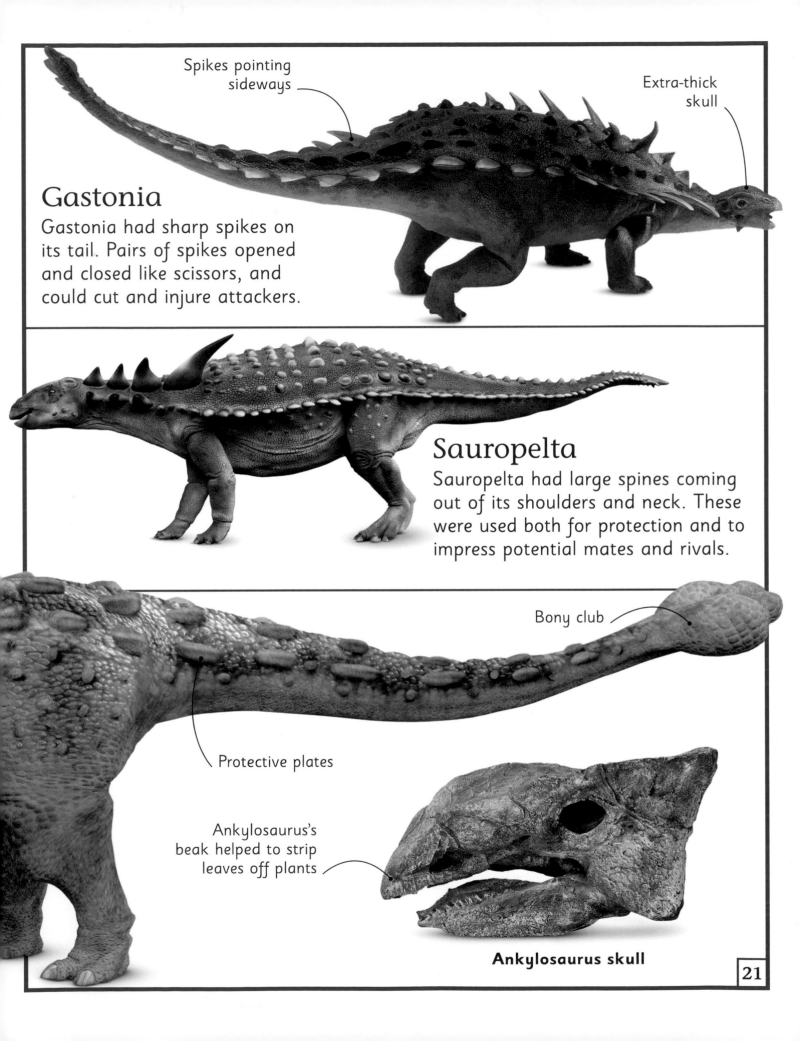

Spikes pointing
sideways

Extra-thick
skull

Gastonia

Gastonia had sharp spikes on
its tail. Pairs of spikes opened
and closed like scissors, and
could cut and injure attackers.

Sauropelta

Sauropelta had large spines coming
out of its shoulders and neck. These
were used both for protection and to
impress potential mates and rivals.

Bony club

Protective plates

Ankylosaurus's
beak helped to strip
leaves off plants

Ankylosaurus skull

21

Plated dinosaurs

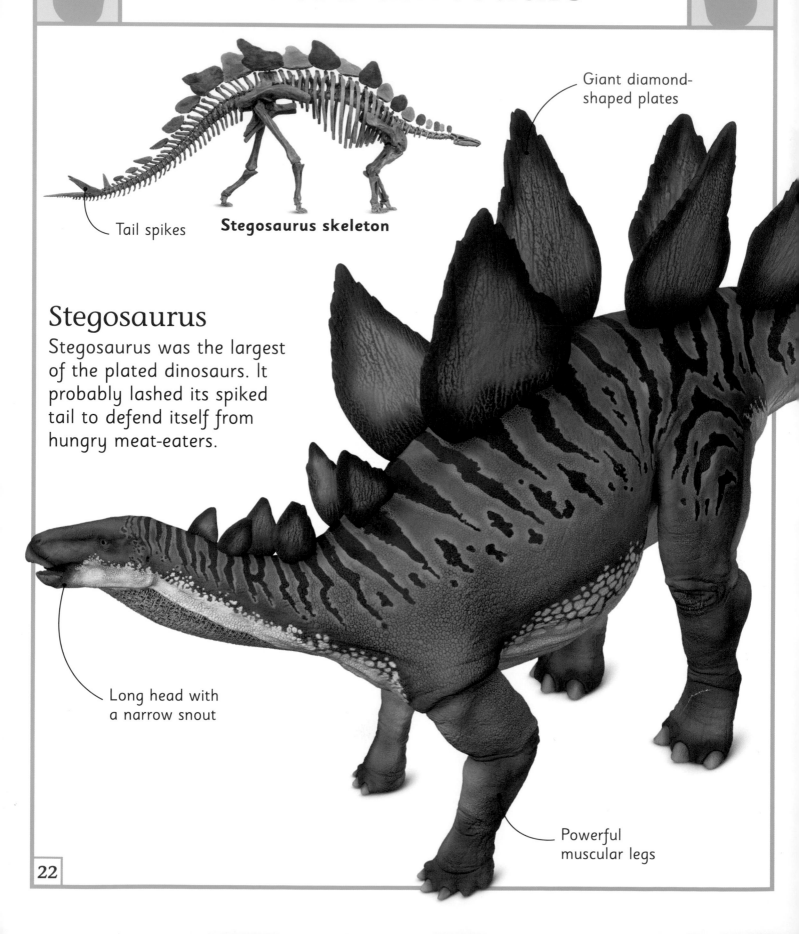

Tail spikes

Stegosaurus skeleton

Giant diamond-shaped plates

Stegosaurus

Stegosaurus was the largest of the plated dinosaurs. It probably lashed its spiked tail to defend itself from hungry meat-eaters.

Long head with a narrow snout

Powerful muscular legs

Kentrosaurus

Kentrosaurus had sharp, pointed spikes that ran along its tail. This plant-eater could whip its tail from side to side to injure its attackers.

Spikes grew from the shoulders

Tuojiangosaurus

Tuojiangosaurus was a dinosaur found in China. It had four sharp spikes on its tail.

Two rows of plates

Beak-like jaws

Huayangosaurus

This dinosaur had small horns on the top of its head, and a short, broad snout. It ate ferns, leaves, and fruit.

Tall, thin plates lined its back

Huge shoulder spike

23

Leaf-eaters

Heterodontosaurus

Heterodontosaurus was small and probably ate leaves and roots. It could run very fast to escape from hungry meat-eating dinosaurs.

Long, rough bristles

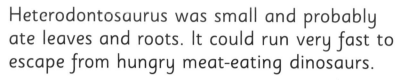

Three long toes on each foot

Claws used to dig in the sand for roots or to tear open insects' nests

Lesothosaurus

Lesothosaurus was not much bigger than a dog. It looked a bit like a lizard that could walk on two legs.

Large eyes

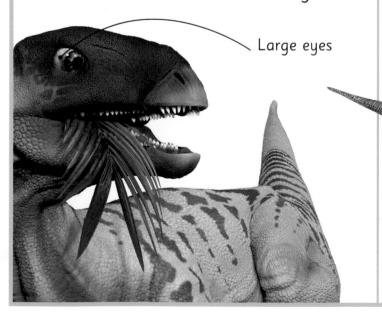

Dryosaurus

Dryosaurus had a turtle-like beak with small teeth, which were used to crush leaves.

Stiff tail

Iguanodon

One of the best-known dinosaurs, Iguanodon was much bigger than many other leaf-eaters. It could probably walk on two legs as well as on all fours.

Toothless beak

Iguanodon skull

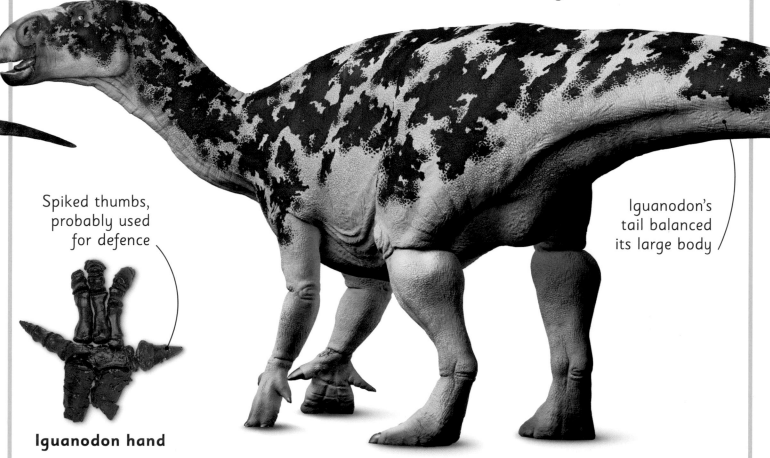

Spiked thumbs, probably used for defence

Iguanodon hand

Iguanodon's tail balanced its large body

Hypsilophodon

Hypsilophodon had big eyes on either side of its head. This gave it an excellent all-around view so it could watch out for danger.

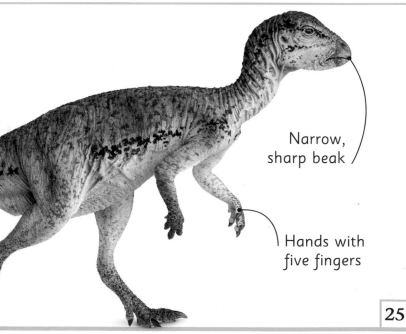

Narrow, sharp beak

Hands with five fingers

Long legs helped Hypsilophodon to run very fast

Duck-billed dinosaurs

Corythosaurus

Corythosaurus means "helmet lizard". It had a thin crest on its head. This was a part of the skull, and was probably used to attract mates.

Ridge along back

Hollow, bony crest

Beak was used for chewing plants

Corythosaurus skull

Gryposaurus

This fossil of Gryposaurus was found in North America. The way the bones fit together show that the tail was held straight out, high off the ground.

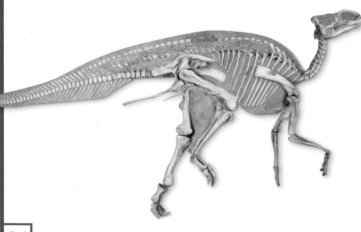

Crest shaped like the blade of an axe

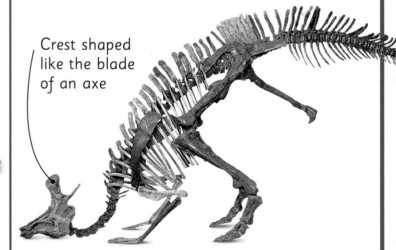

Lambeosaurus

Lambeosaurus had a beak like a duck's, with more than 1,000 teeth used for chewing plants.

Edmontosaurus

Edmontosaurus wandered around in herds. It chewed up tough leaves with its powerful jaws and hundreds of teeth.

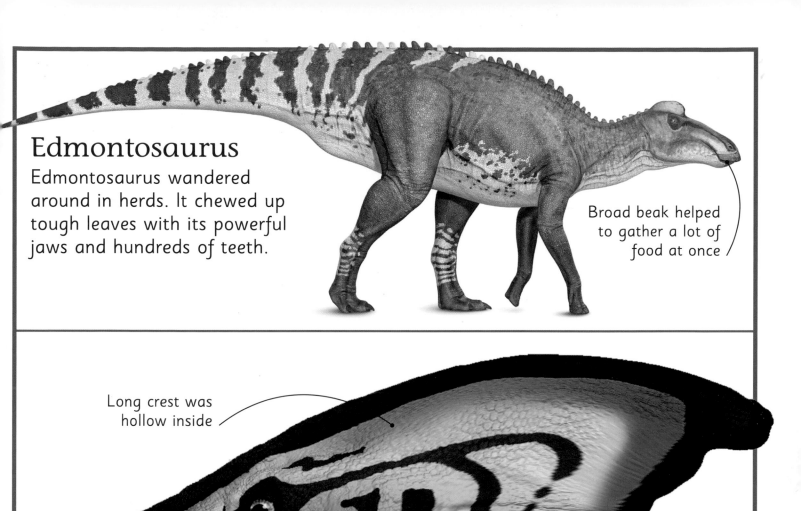

Broad beak helped to gather a lot of food at once

Long crest was hollow inside

Wide, duck-like beak, with grinding teeth to mash up leafy food

Parasaurolophus

Many years ago, some experts thought that Parasaurolophus's crest was used to help it breathe. Now they think it helped the dinosaur to make louder calls.

Boneheads and horns

Styracosaurus

Styracosaurus was a horned-faced dinosaur. It had a head frill with sharp spikes.

Einiosaurus

Einiosaurus had a short frill, with two slim spines growing from the top. This big dinosaur also had a long horn that curved over its snout.

Hooked front horn

Pachycephalosaurus

Pachycephalosaurus had a hard bony head. Experts think these dinosaurs had head-butting contests.

Bony spikes protected the head

Triceratops

Triceratops was like a huge rhinoceros. This plant-eater used its sharp horns to defend itself against meat-eaters.

Short nose horn

Stegoceras

Stegoceras had a bony head shaped like an egg. Its narrow snout had tiny teeth that were used to shred and eat leaves.

Tiny knobs on the head

Protoceratops

Protoceratops was the size of a sheep and had a head frill, but no horns. This small dinosaur may have lived in burrows.

Head frill

Parrot-like beak

Pentaceratops

Pentaceratops means "five-horned face", although this dinosaur had only three horns! There were two on its head and one on its nose. The other two were horn-like growths on its cheeks.

Flying reptiles

Dimorphodon

Dimorphodon was a small reptile that had narrow wings, a large head, and a toothed beak. It hunted insects and small reptiles in woodlands.

Long, bony tail

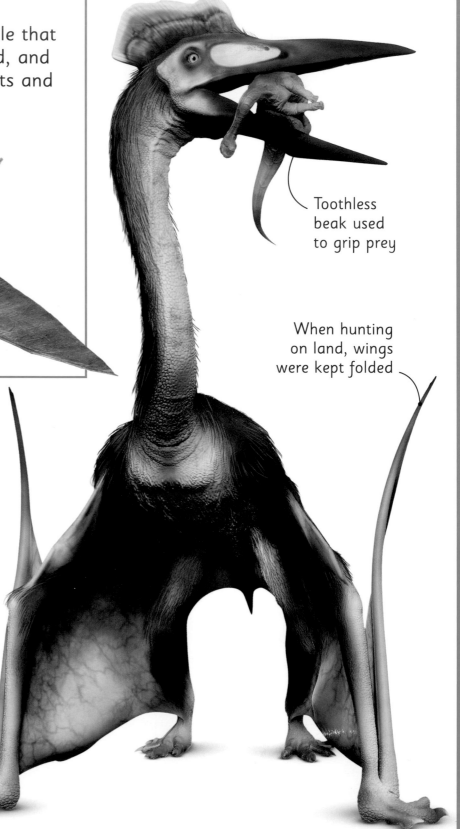

Toothless beak used to grip prey

When hunting on land, wings were kept folded

Quetzalcoatlus

Quetzalcoatlus was one of the largest flying animals that ever lived. It had wings that were 11 m (36 ft) long – almost as long as a school bus. Its giant muscles helped this huge reptile to fly.

Padded hands for walking on the ground

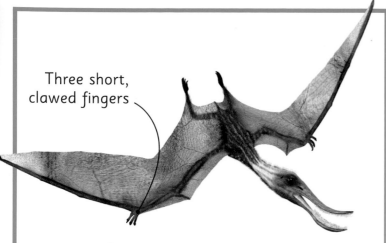

Three short,
clawed fingers

Pterodaustro

Pterodaustro had more than 1,000
teeth, shaped like bristles. It swished
its jaws through the water to catch fish.

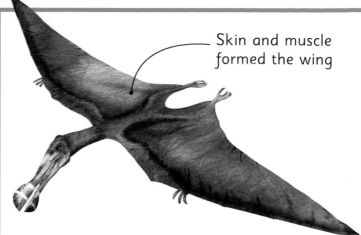

Skin and muscle
formed the wing

Ornithocheirus

Ornithocheirus was the size of a
small aeroplane, with wings about
6 m (20 ft) long.

Pterodactylus had
a long fourth finger
that stretched to the
end of its wing

Pterodactylus

Pterodactylus had a soft crest,
which ran from the top of its snout
to the back of its head. It probably
ate worms and small fish.

Long,
slim legs

Eudimorphodon

This crow-sized reptile had
three fingers, which formed
a "hand" on each wing.

Pterodactylus fossil

A fuzzy coat of very fine
feathers covered its body

Sinosauropteryx

Sinosauropteryx was the first
dinosaur to be found with traces
of feathers. It hunted small animals
such as lizards and insects.

**Microraptor
fossil**

Tuft of feathers

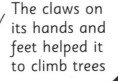

Microraptor

Microraptor was a remarkable
dinosaur with four wings. It had
long feathers on its arms and
legs. These feathers helped it to
glide between trees to look for
prey and escape from enemies.

The claws on
its hands and
feet helped it
to climb trees

Velociraptor

Velociraptor could not fly, but it looked and behaved like an eagle. It ripped apart its prey with the sharp claws on each foot.

Long feathers on arms

Anchiornis

This fully feathered dinosaur weighed less than a crow. Like Microraptor, Anchiornis could glide through the air. It ate small animals such as cockroaches.

Sharp claws

Anchiornis had long arm feathers

Stiff tail feathers

Spinosaurus

Spinosaurus was 17 m (56 ft) long. It had a long, crocodile-like snout and a back shaped like the sail of a boat. It ate fish, small dinosaurs, and flying reptiles, and could probably swim.

Back formed of spine bones

Long, sharp teeth helped catch slippery fish

Irritator

This fish-eater's sail made it look bigger than it was, scaring its enemies. It looked like Spinosaurus, but had a narrower snout.

Baryonyx had 96 teeth

Short muscular arms

Baryonyx

Baryonyx had a long snout and many sharp teeth. It used its giant, hooked claws to scoop fish out of the water.

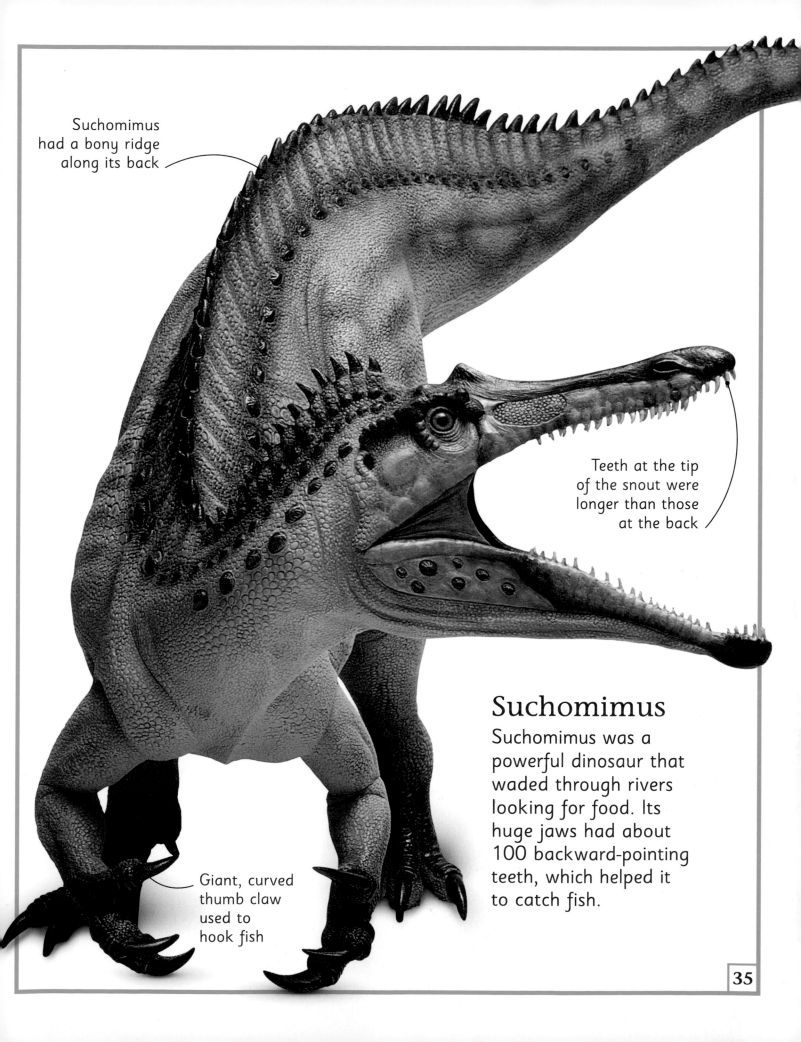

Suchomimus had a bony ridge along its back

Teeth at the tip of the snout were longer than those at the back

Giant, curved thumb claw used to hook fish

Suchomimus

Suchomimus was a powerful dinosaur that waded through rivers looking for food. Its huge jaws had about 100 backward-pointing teeth, which helped it to catch fish.

Marine reptiles

Slender, pointed snout

Tylosaurus

Tylosaurus was a giant sea lizard that was possibly related to snakes. It had a snake-like forked tongue, scaly skin, and big teeth.

Kronosaurus

Kronosaurus was a gigantic marine reptile with a short neck and a big skull. It could tear apart huge animals with its large jaws and sharp teeth.

Spike-like teeth

Lariosaurus

The small Lariosaurus lived mainly in shallow oceans, but often came on land to rest. Its long neck helped it to lunge after fish and shrimps.

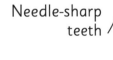

Needle-sharp teeth

Webbed toes

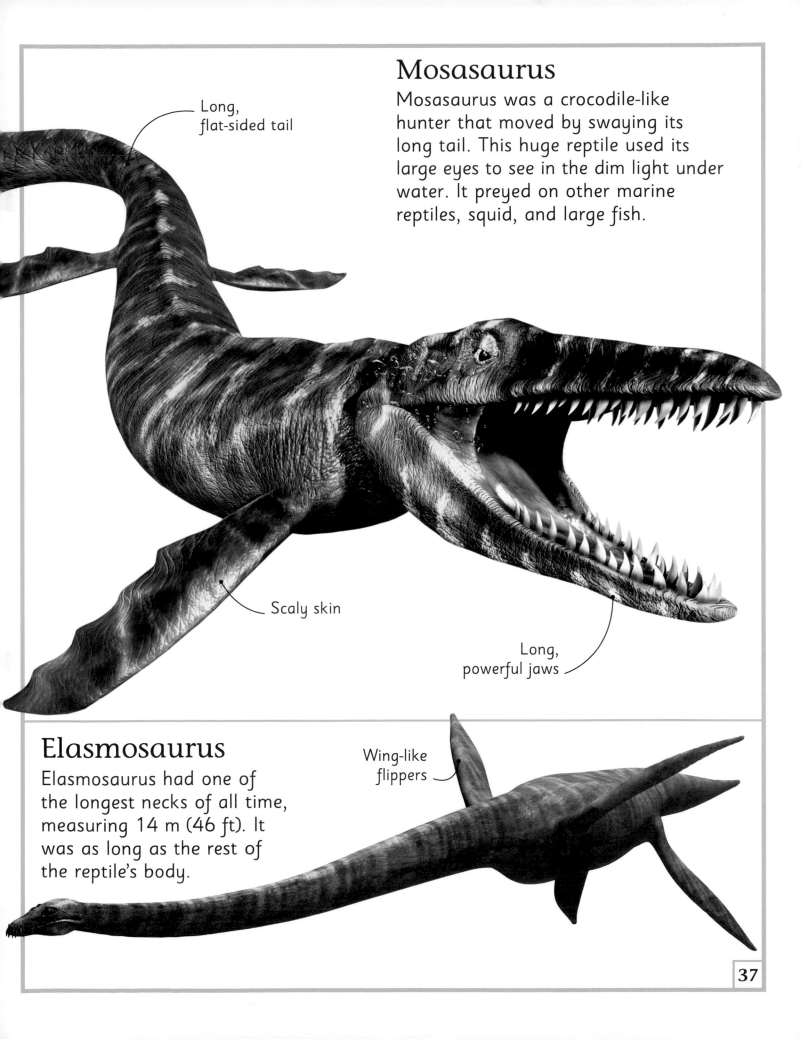

Mosasaurus

Mosasaurus was a crocodile-like hunter that moved by swaying its long tail. This huge reptile used its large eyes to see in the dim light under water. It preyed on other marine reptiles, squid, and large fish.

Long, flat-sided tail

Scaly skin

Long, powerful jaws

Elasmosaurus

Elasmosaurus had one of the longest necks of all time, measuring 14 m (46 ft). It was as long as the rest of the reptile's body.

Wing-like flippers

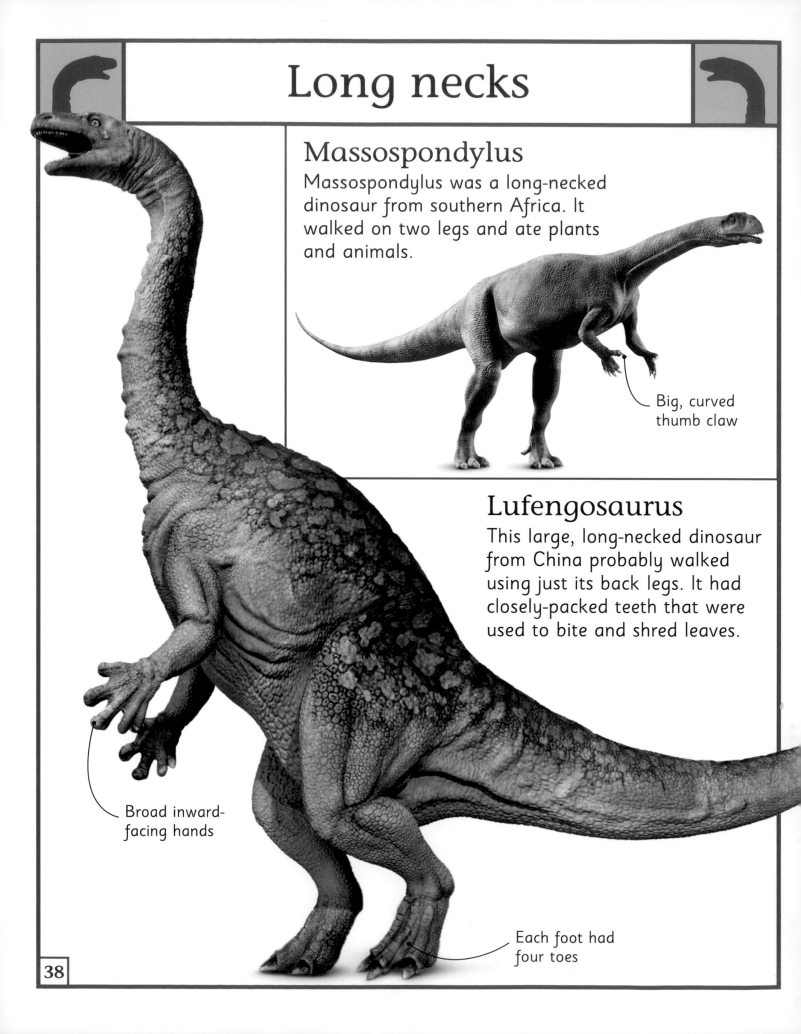

Long necks

Massospondylus

Massospondylus was a long-necked dinosaur from southern Africa. It walked on two legs and ate plants and animals.

Big, curved thumb claw

Lufengosaurus

This large, long-necked dinosaur from China probably walked using just its back legs. It had closely-packed teeth that were used to bite and shred leaves.

Broad inward-facing hands

Each foot had four toes

Thecodontosaurus

Thecodontosaurus was one of the first dinosaurs. Its leg bones suggest it could walk on all fours, as well as on its back legs alone.

Thecodontosaurus's tail was longer than its neck

Plateosaurus

Plateosaurus was one of the biggest dinosaurs of its time, growing up to 10 m (33 ft) long. It used the large curved claws on its hands to fend off predators.

Long, slender neck

Anchisaurus

Anchisaurus was less than 2 m (7 ft) long. It hunted small animals, and one Anchisaurus fossil was found with a lizard in its stomach.

A big, heavy tail helped Plateosaurus to stay balanced

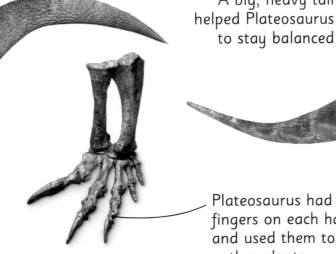

Plateosaurus hand

Plateosaurus had five fingers on each hand, and used them to gather plants

The first birds

Archaeopteryx

Archaeopteryx is one of the earliest known birds. It had a dinosaur-type skeleton, feathers like a modern bird, and small, sharp teeth.

Archaeopteryx had claws on its wings

Long wing feathers

Webbed feet

Vegavis

Vegavis was a bird from Antarctica. Scientists think it was an early member of the duck family.

Ichthyornis

Ichthyornis was a seabird that was the size of a gull. It had a long beak with sharp, curved teeth, which helped it grab small and slippery fish.

Long tail streamers

Clawed feet

Iberomesornis

Iberomesornis was the size of a sparrow and probably ate insects and other small animals. The muscles it used for flying were not as strong as the muscles of today's birds.

Feet adapted for perching

Strong beak

Clawed, three-fingered hand

Confuciusornis

Confuciusornis was one of the first birds with a toothless beak. It lived in China and had large hand claws, which probably helped it to move through trees. Its four-toed feet were used to perch on branches.

Outer wing feathers were as long as those of modern birds

Dinosaur nursery

Nesting together

Dinosaurs laid eggs, as do reptiles and birds. Scientists have found fossils of eggs, nests, and babies belonging to duck-billed dinosaurs called Maiasaura. Female dinosaurs built their nests close together for safety and looked after their babies once the eggs had hatched.

Maiasaura's eggs were pear-shaped and about the size of a child's head

The nests were mounds of earth hollowed out in the middle

Protecting the young

Fossil footprints of the big plant-eaters show that they travelled in herds. The adults protected the younger dinosaurs, as elephants do today with their young.

Meat-eating dinosaur attacking plant-eaters

Young dinosaurs joined herds once they were half as big as adults

Saltasaurus eggs

Saltasaurus eggs were round and the size of small melons. Once these hatched, the tiny babies were probably fed by their parents.

Protoceratops

Protoceratops laid eggs that looked like big potatoes. These were laid in shallow pits made in the sand. The babies were about 20 cm (8 in) long when they hatched.

Nanotyrannus

Dinosaurs changed a lot as they grew, which sometimes makes identifying new species tricky. The predator Nanotyrannus was once thought to be a separate species. Now experts think it was actually a young Tyrannosaurus rex.

Like T. rex, Nanotyrannus had rows of sharp teeth

Nanotyrannus skull

Nanotyrannus had small arms, like Tyrannosaurus rex

Nanotyrannus was 6 m (20 ft) long, about half the length of T. rex

Tyrannosaurus rex skull

Torosaurus

For years scientists thought that Torosaurus was a species related to Triceratops. However, some dinosaur experts now think Torosaurus could be an old adult Triceratops that has grown a super-long frill.

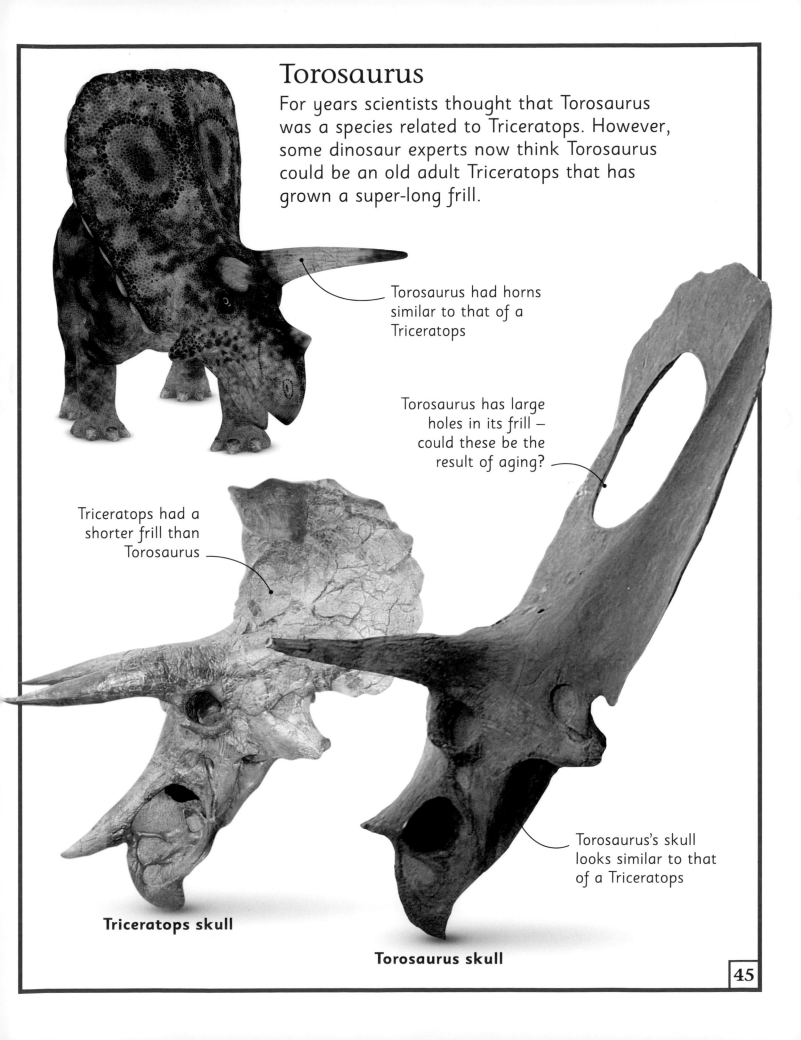

Torosaurus had horns similar to that of a Triceratops

Torosaurus has large holes in its frill – could these be the result of aging?

Triceratops had a shorter frill than Torosaurus

Torosaurus's skull looks similar to that of a Triceratops

Triceratops skull

Torosaurus skull

In scale

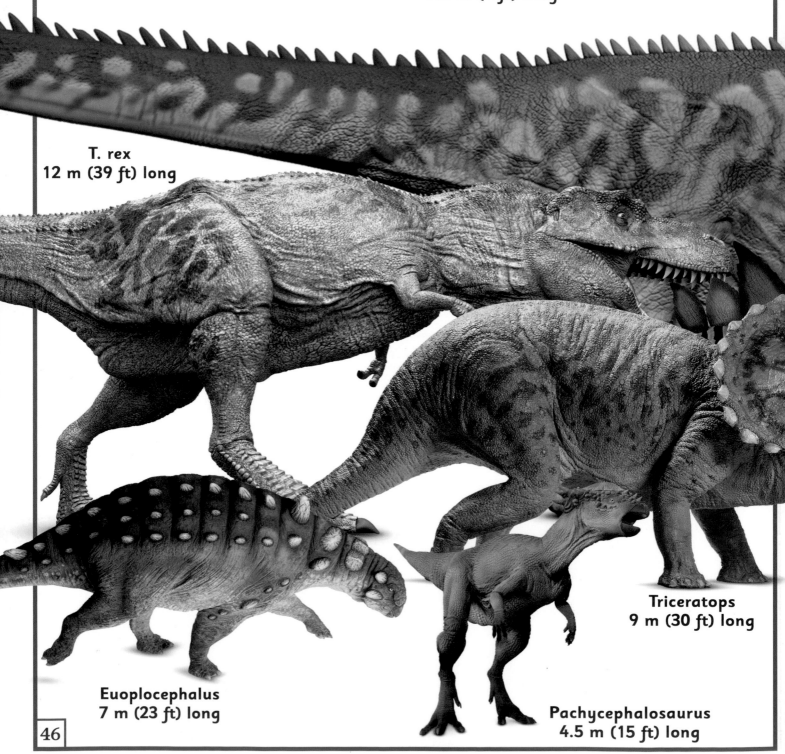

Pterodaustro
2.5 m (8 ft) long

T. rex
12 m (39 ft) long

Triceratops
9 m (30 ft) long

Euoplocephalus
7 m (23 ft) long

Pachycephalosaurus
4.5 m (15 ft) long

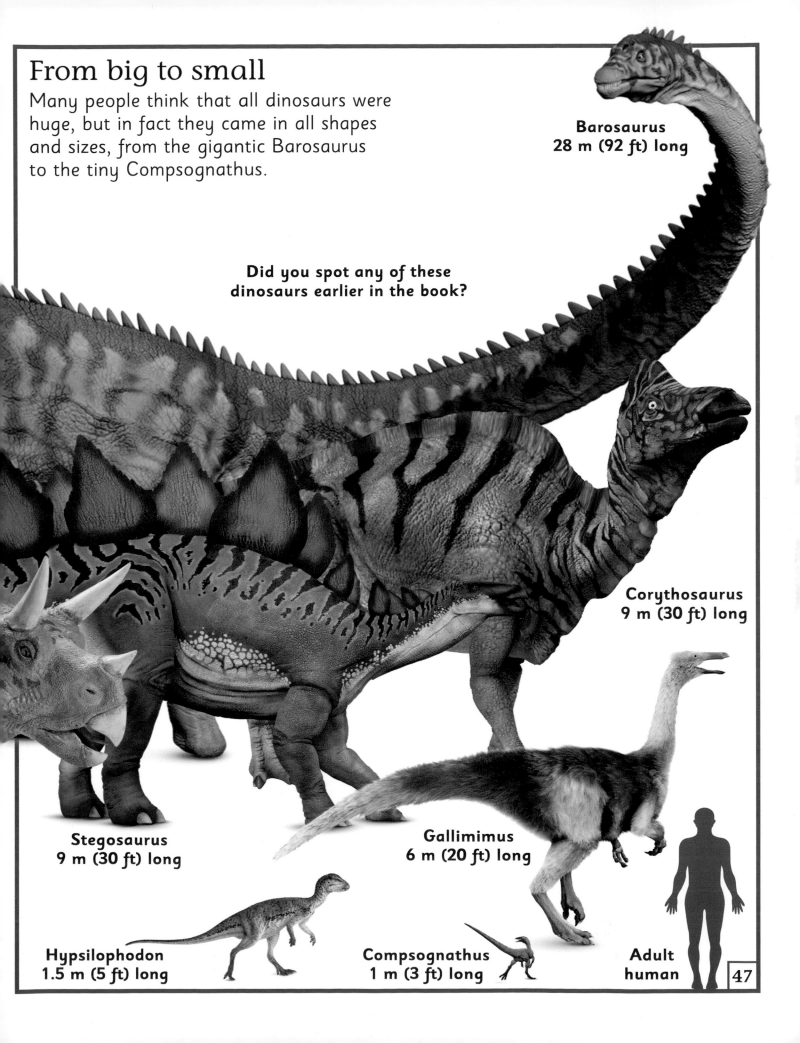

From big to small

Many people think that all dinosaurs were huge, but in fact they came in all shapes and sizes, from the gigantic Barosaurus to the tiny Compsognathus.

Barosaurus
28 m (92 ft) long

Did you spot any of these dinosaurs earlier in the book?

Corythosaurus
9 m (30 ft) long

Stegosaurus
9 m (30 ft) long

Gallimimus
6 m (20 ft) long

Hypsilophodon
1.5 m (5 ft) long

Compsognathus
1 m (3 ft) long

Adult human

47

Index